Female Eastern Bluebird

Male Eastern Bluebird

Birds that are blue have been a symbol of happiness around the world for thousands of years. They have appeared in poems, art, songs, films, folktales, and myths.

The United States is home to a particular group of blue birds that includes Eastern, Mountain, and Western Bluebirds. E. Bluebird, the narrator of this book, is an Eastern Bluebird. She is based on a bird the author observed in his backyard in Connecticut where she and her mate raised five chicks.

Bluebirds are beloved for their bright blue coloring and, for people in the north, as welcome signs of spring. The female adult Eastern Bluebird is grayer in color than the bright blue male.

Not all Bluebirds migrate. Some Bluebirds that live in warm places stay there year-round. In September or the beginning of October, the Eastern Bluebirds that do migrate join flocks that fly south to warmer climates where they find more to eat. They travel to the Carolinas and other southern states. Some Eastern Bluebirds migrate as far as Nicaragua.

In January and February, migrating Eastern Bluebirds begin their trip north. Many reach their breeding sites in February or early March, but those that fly to Canada may arrive in early May.

Eastern Bluebird Migration

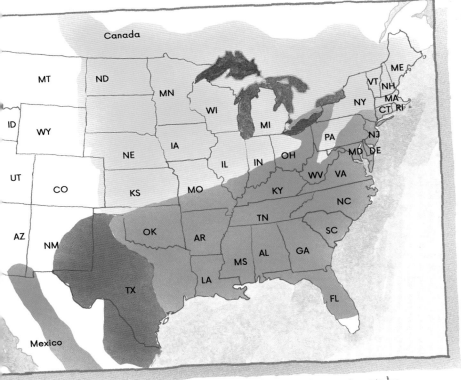

Yellow is the summer range only.
Green is where Eastern Bluebirds are found year-round.
Purple is where they live in winter only.

In early spring, a Bluebird couple looks for a place to build a nest, such as a hole in a tree or a human-made nest box. The female does most of the building while the male stands guard. Bluebirds use grasses, small sticks, pine needles, and feathers. Nest building takes two to six days. An Eastern Bluebird like E. Bluebird will usually have two broods in one season.

Eastern Bluebirds prefer open spaces, like fields or meadows, with trees nearby. Bluebirds, which like to perch on branches and watch for insects moving on the ground, have very good eyesight and can see small insects as far as fifty feet away.

Bluebirds eat grasshoppers, crickets, katydids, beetles, spiders, millipedes, centipedes, saw bugs, and snails. They also eat wild fruits and berries, especially in colder weather when there are fewer insects.

In the wild, Bluebirds are cavity nesters. Cavity nesters live in holes in trees created by decay or by other birds, such as Woodpeckers. Competition for nests from nonnative cavity nesters (especially House Sparrows and European Starlings), loss of woodland, and predators (raccoons that eat eggs and baby birds, for example) caused Bluebird populations to decline sharply from the late 1800s to the 1960s.

E. Bluebird's house is human-made and not a natural tree cavity. In the 1970s, people began providing Bluebird houses. Because of this, the number of Bluebirds has been increasing in recent years.

My Happy Year

by E. Bluebird

PAUL MEISEL

Holiday House ❦ New York

For all bird and nature lovers

The publisher thanks Dr. Daniel Leger and Dr. Paul R. Sweet
for reviewing this book.

Library of Congress Cataloging-in-Publication Data

Names: Meisel, Paul, author, illustrator.
Title: My happy year by E. Bluebird / Paul Meisel.
Description: First edition. | New York : Holiday House, [2019]
Audience: Ages 4-8. | Audience: K to grade 3.
Identifiers: LCCN 2018001857 | ISBN 9780823438372 (hardcover)
Subjects: LCSH: Eastern bluebird—Juvenile literature. | CYAC: Bluebirds.
Classification: LCC QL696.P288 M4325 2019 | DDC 598.8/42—dc23
LC record available at https://lccn.loc.gov/2018001857

ISBN: 978-0-8234-4678-0 (paperback)

JUNE 1

Today is my birthday! I can't see yet. When I stick my head up and open my beak, Mom and Dad feed me.

JUNE 2

It feels like there are other little birds around me.
Mom stays with us to keep us warm when she's not
getting food.

JUNE 4

I still can't see. Eating lots of bugs. I'm growing fast!

JUNE 6

I can see now! And there are three other baby birds.

We eat almost all day long.

Beetles, crickets, caterpillars, grasshoppers, moths, spiders. Yum!

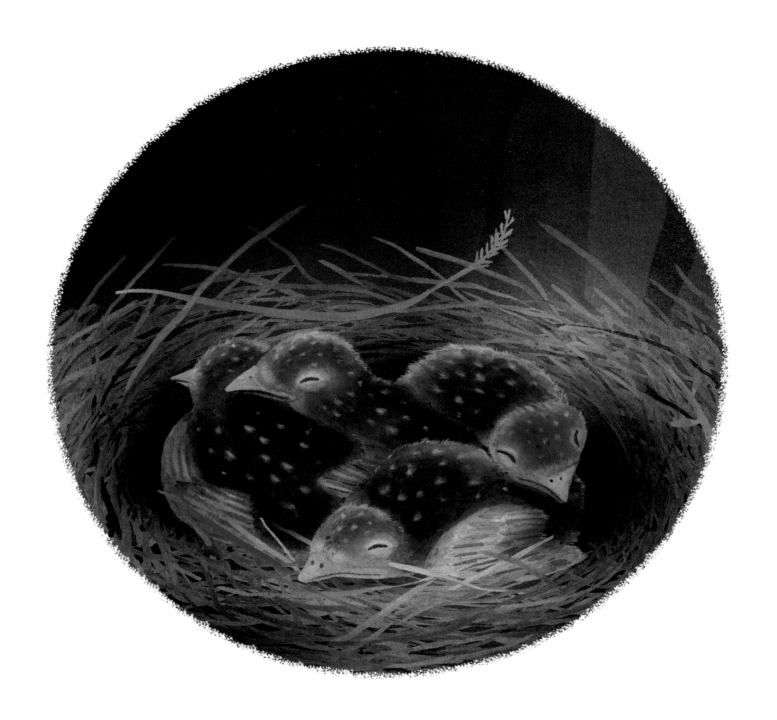

JUNE 7

Mom isn't sleeping with us anymore. Some feathers
are starting to grow. I can see my wings! At night we
sleep close to stay warm.

JUNE 9

Eating all these bugs makes me poop.
Mom takes my poop sack out of the nest.
Good thing. It gets pretty yucky in here.

JUNE 14

I have real wings now. The others are talking about leaving the nest. I like it in here. It's safe.

A big bird comes by and looks inside. He's too big to reach us, so he flies away. Phew! He looked hungry!

JUNE 18

It's getting too crowded. One of us is ready to leave.

He hops to the hole and jumps.

He flaps his wings and
falls to the ground.
Mom tells him to get up
and fly.

He flaps some more and flies to the
branch where Dad is.
WOW!

JUNE 19

The others leave the nest too. They flap and flap and fly up into a tree. I don't want to leave yet. I'm afraid.

JUNE 20

I can see Mom and Dad feeding my siblings up in a tree.
Mom comes to feed me too. She wants me to leave
the nest, but I still don't want to.

JUNE 21

Where's my family?
I can hear them singing,
but I can't see them.

I'm hungry, but Mom hasn't
come with any food.
Okay. It's time to be brave.

I stand in the hole, take a
deep breath, and jump!
I flap and flap . . . I'm flying!

I land in a tree.

My family comes
to see me.

JULY 4

Flying is amazing! Through the trees, over the meadows and streams. Everything is so beautiful from up here.

SEPTEMBER 14

Fall is coming. Mom tells me that it's time to go someplace warm.

SEPTEMBER 28

I see a flock of Bluebirds. We're going south! I catch up with my family just in time.

OCTOBER 4

So much flying! We stop to rest. Luckily there are more bugs here than back home. Then we're on our way again.

OCTOBER 7

We made it! It's warm and sunny. Lots of tasty bugs.
Cats too. I have to be careful.

FEBRUARY 27

Months have passed. The days are getting longer.
Guess what! It's time to travel back
north. A flock of Bluebirds gathers,
and we're off.

MARCH 12

I'm home! It's still cold out, but there are lots of berries to eat.

APRIL 29

It's getting warmer. Time
to look for a mate.

I find one! And he picks a pretty house for us.

MAY 15

I build a nest out of grass
while he guards the house.

MAY 22

I lay five perfect blue eggs. I sit on them. In a couple of weeks, my chicks will hatch.

JUNE 4

Look at my beautiful chicks!
I'm so happy!

European Starling

House Sparrow

GLOSSARY

Brood: (noun) a family of young birds produced at one hatching; (verb) to sit on eggs to hatch them

Chick: a newly hatched bird

Fledgling: a young bird that has developed wing feathers capable of flight

Migrate: to move from one habitat (or region) to another according to the seasons

You can learn more about Bluebirds at these websites:

Bluebird Restoration Association of Wisconsin (http://www.braw.org)

The Cornell Lab of Ornithology (https://www.allaboutbirds.org)

chick

If you want to build your own Bluebird house, there are many good plans available on the internet. Here are two:

http://www.audubon.org/news/diy-build-bluebird-box (National Audubon Society)

http://www.ct.gov/deep/cwp/view.asp?a=2723&q=325966 (State of Connecticut Department of Energy and Environmental Protection)

Fledgling

"*Tu-a-wee*" is the most common song of Eastern Bluebirds. Males usually have a loud song that goes "*tury, cherwee, cheye-le*" or "*aye ala loee— alee ay lalo leeo.*" Females can sing the same song, often in a softer version. Bluebirds make many other sounds—screeches, screams, squawks, chirps, turrs, chatter, and rasps, depending on the situation. You can learn more about the sounds of Eastern Bluebirds at the Cornell Lab of Ornithology website (https://www.allaboutbirds.org/guide/ Eastern_Bluebird/sounds).

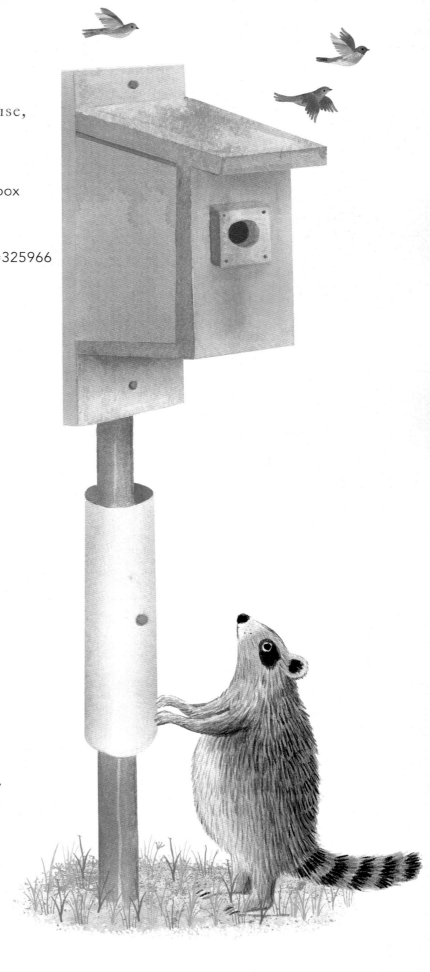